KT-217-725

FOR THE LOVE OF
DOGS

FOR THE LOVE OF DOGS

First published in 2015 as *Dogs: A Miscellany*
This revised and updated edition copyright © Summersdale Publishers
Ltd, 2017

With research by Vicky Edwards

Illustrations © Shutterstock

Summersdale Publishers Ltd
46 West Street
Chichester
West Sussex
PO19 1RP
UK

www.summersdale.com

Printed and bound in the Czech Republic

ISBN: 978-1-78685-032-4

Substantial discounts on bulk quantities of Summersdale books are available
to corporations, professional associations and other organisations. For
details contact general enquiries: telephone: +44 (0) 1243 771107, fax:
+44 (0) 1243 786300 or email: enquiries@summersdale.com

FOR THE LOVE OF
DOGS

KATE MAY

summersdale

CONTENTS

INTRODUCTION

Intelligent, loyal, affectionate, great fun and brilliant walking buddies – there's a lot to love about dogs. From those that sniff out disease and bombs to those four-legged superstars who support the blind, deaf and disabled by acting as their eyes, ears and mobility, dogs are far more than pets to those who depend on them.

As long-standing inspiration for artists and writers, dogs are also celebrated in literature, art, film, television and song. Their cute factor also makes them a marketeer's dream, which is why some of the world's most memorable advertising campaigns feature dogs.

And for many, dogs truly are man's or woman's best friend. Always willing to cock an ear and listen to your woes, or let you cuddle up to them for comfort, they are our confidantes as well as our companions, truly a part of our family.

Whether you are a dog owner or just a dog lover, this book is a salute to pups, pedigrees and mutts the world over. I hope that it will cheer, inform and entertain in equal measure.

HISTORY: FROM WOLF TO MAN'S BEST FRIEND

For the strength of the Pack is the Wolf, and the strength of the Wolf is the Pack.

RUDYARD KIPLING

There has been much debate over the years about the precise origins of our modern-day pooches. Scientists agree that dogs are directly descended from *Canis lupus* – or, as it is more commonly known, the grey wolf – but until recently the timing and exact whereabouts of their evolution was as woolly as an Old English Sheepdog's winter coat.

Early DNA studies on samples dating back some 18,000 years suggested that the modern-day dog evolved from wolves that were integrated into human societies in the Middle East, or possibly in East Asia, as recently as 15,000 years ago. However, in 2013, new research unveiled in *Science* magazine gave us a clearer insight. Genetic analysis of dog and wolf samples, both ancient and modern, suggested that modern dogs are actually more closely related to ancient European canines than to any of the farther flung wolf groups.

DEVELOPMENT

The latest data suggests that dogs were domesticated far earlier than previously thought. Research undertaken by Dr Olaf Thalmann at Finland's University of Turku concluded that dogs started to evolve from wolves at a time when humankind had yet to form settlements and was still sourcing food by hunting.

Because dog populations have become very mixed over time, evolving into numerous different breeds and crossbreeds and settling all over the world, it is difficult for scientists to reach a definite conclusion. To do this, further sampling, analysis and research is needed.

DON'T BITE THE HAND THAT FEEDS YOU

Researchers and scientists have turned their focus to the question of how dogs came to be domesticated. One credible possibility is that wolves would follow hunters, probably at a distance, feasting on the scraps and carcasses left over after big kills. From here, perhaps the wolves grew braver and came closer, possibly with hunters encouraging them with titbits, thinking to use the wolves' acute hearing to warn them when bigger predators such as bears were near, and perhaps also to use their furry bodies as prehistoric duvets.

GETTING TO KNOW YOU

Wolves may also have been encouraged into settlements when humans realised that wolves ate rats and other pests, as well as waste. No waste meant fewer flies and fewer flies meant less sickness, making groups that 'embraced' the wolves healthier and hardier than those that chased them away. Another theory is that wolf cubs proved easy to tame and that orphaned wolf pups may have been adopted into human groups. Either way, the fearsome pack animal slowly but surely became a submissive servant to its hunter master.

DID YOU KNOW?

The dog family (Canidae) contains all fox, wolf, coyote, jackal and dog-like mammals. Wild canids are found on every continent, with the exception of Antarctica.

DID YOU KNOW?

The expression 'three-dog night' was first coined by the Inuit to describe a particularly cold night, when only the body heat of three dogs could keep you warm.

Recollect that the Almighty, who gave the dog to be companion of our pleasures and our toils, hath invested him with a nature noble and incapable of deceit.

SIR WALTER SCOTT

DOMESTICATION AND DEVELOPMENT

Researchers believe that the domestication of dogs happened over a period of many hundreds of years, as they were gradually bred for specific roles.

Hunting was obviously the principal role for which dogs were used, leading to breeding that accentuated particular traits such as sense of smell, speed and agility, size (small enough to follow quarry into its habitat, for instance), stamina and herding instinct.

But in ancient times, up to and including the Middle Ages, very few people were wealthy enough to feed a dog as we do today. Instead, dogs had to scavenge for their own food, often living on a diet of rats. Only working dogs – sled-pullers or herding dogs – would have been given food. Hunting dogs were often given scraps from their conquests, but most others were entirely self-sufficient. As a result of such a diet they were often undernourished and prone to disease and infestation.

LEADER OF THE PACK TO FAITHFUL SERVANT

It is probable that, once adopted into a human group, dogs lost their canine pack instinct and instead integrated themselves into the family groups of hunters. Perhaps this is how humans began to interact with dogs on a one-to-one basis, and thus how the close relationships we have with our pet dogs today began.

One of the earliest indications that humans and dogs enjoyed a shared affection can be traced to the burial site of a woman in Israel. Dating back to approximately 11,000 BP (before present), the woman's hand is placed on a dog which has been buried with her. Similarly, at the earliest cemetery in Skateholm, Sweden (dating back to 5,000 BCE – before current era), there is evidence that dogs were sometimes buried with people. It is likely that these dogs were sacrificed to accompany their masters or mistresses on their journey to the afterlife. The excavation of Egyptian tombs has also revealed that dogs were mummified and buried with their masters. Some dogs were even given their own grave. Buried also with hunting tools, it suggests they were highly valued as hunting dogs.

POSH PAWS AND PETS

From the latter part of the Middle Ages, hunting and hawking became favourite sports of the upper echelons of society. Wealthy and keen for their dogs to do better than those belonging to their fellow sportsmen, it was around this time that dogs started to be treated more as pets.

Performing dogs became a much-loved source of entertainment, with jesters and fools including them in their routines. From hunting to herding, over time this increased integration with human beings taught dogs a great deal about what was expected and wanted of them. And, as more civilised times came to pass, our canine friends continued to evolve.

A FAVOURED BREED

One breed that has survived, albeit only just, since earliest times is the Vizsla, or Hungarian Pointer. Originally the dog of the Magyar tribes that invaded Central Europe during the Dark Ages, etchings depicting a Magyar warrior and a dog resembling a Vizsla date back to the early tenth century. Later adopted by Hungarian nobility, the breed all but became extinct after World War One, only surviving thanks to the efforts of Vizsla fanciers. During World War Two, many Hungarians fled the Russian occupation, taking their Vizslas with them. Vizslas reappeared in the 1950s, and the breed was recognised by the American Kennel Club in 1960.

If a dog will not come to you after having looked you in the face, you should go home and examine your conscience.

WOODROW WILSON

EUROPE: A CONTINENT OF PET LOVERS

75 million	Number of European households owning at least one pet animal
45 per cent	Estimated percentage of European households owning at least one cat or dog
80,002,940	Number of pet dogs living in Europe
15,894,000	Russia has the biggest pet dog population in Europe
8,500,000	The UK has the second biggest pet dog population in Europe

BREEDING NOTES

The Dobermann Pinscher was first bred by Louis Dobermann, a tax collector. Evidently he bred the dog specifically to frighten people into paying their dues.

Also known as 'Aussiepoo', the Aussiedoodle is a Poodle–Australian Shepherd cross.

The Chinese Crested breed comes in two varieties: the Hairless and the Powderpuff.

The Golden Retriever originates from Scotland. During the 1860s Sir Dudley Marjoribanks mated a yellow Retriever with a Tweed Water Spaniel. The result was the first 'goldie'.

Capable of a top speed of up to 72 kilometres per hour (45 miles per hour), the Greyhound is the world's fastest dog.

The Jack Russell Terrier has a bark that is certainly as big as its bite. Given its diminutive stature, this dog has a disproportionately loud voice!

To breed a St Dane you need to cross a Great Dane with a St Bernard.

Legend says that the Pekingese, one of the world's oldest dog breeds and once held sacred by emperors, was the result of a liaison between a lion and a monkey.

The Newfoundland dog was originally bred to help fishermen drag in their nets and to rescue people from drowning. Often called upon to 'doggy paddle', this incredible hound is blessed with a water-resistant coat and webbed feet.

Chow Chows are known for their distinctive blue-black tongues. At birth, however, they have pink tongues. The change from pink to black takes place between eight and ten weeks of age.

Bred in Germany centuries ago to hunt badgers, the Dachshund's name means 'badger dog'.

With a natural and heavily ingrained tendency to chase and kill anything that it regards as prey, smaller domestic pets will never be able to relax if they live with a Jack Russell.

LOYAL TO PRINCE LLEWELYN

In the village of Beddgelert, northwest Wales, a tribute to a brave and faithful hound is engraved on the supposed grave of Gelert, the famed favourite hunting dog of Prince Llewelyn. It reads:

> *In the thirteenth century Llewelyn, Prince of North Wales, had a palace at Beddgelert. One day he went hunting without Gelert, 'The Faithful Hound', who was unaccountably absent. On Llewelyn's return the truant, stained and smeared with blood, joyfully sprang to meet his master. The prince, alarmed, hastened to find his son, and saw the infant's cot empty, the bedclothes and floor covered with blood. The frantic father plunged the sword into the hound's side, thinking it had killed his heir. The dog's dying yell was answered by a child's cry. Llewelyn searched and discovered his boy unharmed, but nearby lay the body of a mighty wolf which Gelert had slain. The prince, filled with remorse, is said never to have smiled again. He buried Gelert here. The spot is called Beddgelert.'*

ROYAL DOGS

Queen of France Marie Antoinette was, by all accounts, very fond of her Spaniel, Thisbe; loyal and faithful Caesar, a Terrier belonging to King Edward VII, walked behind His Majesty's coffin in the funeral procession; and Queen Elizabeth II continues the long-standing royal affection for dogs. Royal canines span a wide variety of breeds, but it is the Corgi that most people associate with our present queen. First introduced to royal life by King George VI in 1933 when he acquired Dookie, which delighted the young princesses Elizabeth and Margaret, Dookie was joined soon by another Corgi named Jane, whose puppies, Crackers and Carol, also became part of the royal household. One of the Queen's favourite Corgis was Susan, who was an eighteenth birthday present.

I dressed dear sweet little Dash for the second time after dinner in a scarlet jacket and blue trousers.

**QUEEN VICTORIA, ON HER PET
CAVALIER KING CHARLES SPANIEL**

*Here lies DASH, the Favourite Spaniel
of Queen Victoria.
By whose command this Memorial was erected.
He died on the 20 December, 1840
in his 9th year.
His attachment was without selfishness,
His playfulness without malice,
His fidelity without deceit.
READER, if you would live beloved and die
regretted, profit by the example of DASH.*

EPITAPH ON DASH'S GRAVESTONE

DID YOU KNOW?

In 1393 the Duke of Berry, a member of the French royal family, was so touched by a dog that refused to leave its master's grave that he provided funds to keep the loyal hound fed for the rest of its days.

DID YOU KNOW?

The Old Mother Hubbard of the nursery rhyme is said to be Cardinal Wolsey, chief statesman and churchman of English Tudor history. Wolsey angered King Henry VIII when he failed to obtain the king's divorce from Catherine of Aragon. Henry was keen to divorce Catherine so that he could marry Anne Boleyn. In the famous rhyme, Henry was represented by the 'doggie'. The 'bone' was the divorce, while the 'cupboard' was symbolic of the Catholic Church.

During the Prince's visit, King Timahoe will be referred to only as Timahoe, since it would be inappropriate for the Prince to be outranked by a dog.

IN CORRESPONDENCE BETWEEN RICHARD M. NIXON AND WHITE HOUSE STAFF ON HOW TO ADDRESS THE PRESIDENT'S IRISH SETTER, KING TIMAHOE, DURING A VISIT BY PRINCE CHARLES

SIGNIFICANT DATES RELATING TO BREEDING AND PEDIGREE

3,000–4,000 years ago: first breeding for purpose. Greyhounds and Mastiffs were the first developed breeds; Greyhounds bred for speed and Mastiffs for protection

Middle Ages: dogs first bred specifically for their hunting abilities

1570: first known attempt at classifying dogs by Dr John Caius in *De Canibus Britannicis*

1770: The Clumber Spaniel, largest of the English sporting Spaniels, is bred for the first time at Clumber Park, Nottinghamshire, England

1873: The Kennel Club is founded in the UK

1884: The American Kennel Club is founded

1891: Charles Cruft stages the first Crufts dog show at the Royal Agricultural Hall, Islington, London with 2,437 entries and 36 breeds attending

A dog is the only thing on earth that loves you more than he loves himself.

JOSH BILLINGS

BARK WHEN YOUR BREED IS CALLED OUT

There are 360 official dog breeds worldwide, although there are many more which aren't formally recognised (different countries have different criteria for the recognition of different breeds).

A description of the traits and features of every breed are laid down by organisations such as the UK's Kennel Club, including so-called 'designer' dogs, like the Puggle, which is a cross between a Pug and a Beagle.

The Kennel Club UK has agreements with over 40 Kennel Clubs around the world. Other similar organisations around the globe also manage breed registers. In most instances, new breeds are considered for recognition once there are specimens of it in its country of origin.

I wonder if other dogs think poodles are members of a weird religious cult.

RITA RUDNER

List of clubs with which The Kennel Club has full reciprocal agreements outside the UK

Australia	Guernsey	Philippines
Austria	Hong Kong	Portugal
Barbados	Iceland	San Marino
Belgium	Ireland	Singapore
Bermuda	Italy	South Africa
Brazil	Luxembourg	Spain
Canada	Jamaica	Sri Lanka
Chile	Jersey	Sweden
Colombia	Korea	Switzerland
Cyprus	Malaysia	Trinidad
Denmark	Malta*	Tobago
East Africa	Monaco	Uruguay
Finland	Nepal	USA
France	Netherlands	Zambia
Germany	New Zealand	Zimbabwe
Gibraltar	Norway	
Greece	Pakistan	

* Malta has a provisional reciprocal agreement

THE LANGUAGE OF DOGS

The expression 'black dog' to describe depression, conjures up a powerful image: a dark and shadowy figure that lurks; an ever-present but unwelcome guest that, if it were to pounce, would destroy one. A figure long since associated with fear, in folklore and myth, black dogs in dreams are thought to represent death. Famously referred to by Sir Winston Churchill, twice prime minister of the UK, to describe his bouts of gloom, the expression is now common parlance and is often used to articulate a feeling of downheartedness, inexplicable sadness or negativity.

COLLECTIVE CANINES

Kennel: dogs in general
Cowardice: curs and mongrels
Pack, cry or mute: Hounds
Litter: puppies
Pack: wild dogs

Buy a pup and your money will buy love unflinching that cannot lie.

RUDYARD KIPLING

SHOWING OFF AND RECORD BREAKERS

Anybody who doesn't know
what soap tastes like never
washed a dog.

FRANKLIN P. JONES

GIFTED PUPS

Today our dogs' achievements are documented and celebrated via social and traditional media. From 'Best in Show' to the dog who can balance a stack of steaks on his nose, we humans love to watch our canine friends and to read about their talents.

DOG SHOWS AND COMPETITIONS

Bred to work, it wasn't until the middle of the 1800s that dogs began to be appreciated for their appearance and personalities rather than merely their strength or speed. In 1859, Setters and Pointers and their humans were invited to what is believed to be the first formal dog show in the world, held in Newcastle upon Tyne in northeast England. Over the next decade there was a huge swell of popularity in the hobby of showing off one's dog, and the idea was quickly picked up in America. However, due to the Civil War, America didn't host its first dog show until 1877. Today dog shows take place all over the world, with some dogs travelling the globe like superstars as they collect piece after piece of silverware.

CRUFTS

One of the most famous dog shows in the world is Crufts, now held at the National Exhibition Centre in Birmingham. The brainchild of Charles Cruft, it is now one of the biggest and most prestigious dog events in the world. Much more than just a competition, Crufts today celebrates dogs in every conceivable sense – as workers, pedigrees, performers and more. It is a vast festival that attracts crowds of exhibitors and spectators and, whether you are a wannabe dog owner, a dog lover or you take your dog to participate, Crufts is a paradise for all things canine.

CRUFTS HISTORY

Crufts is named after its founder, Charles Cruft. Leaving college in 1876 Charles accepted a job with James Spratt who had opened a shop in London selling his newly dreamed-up confection: dog cakes.

In 1886, Cruft took over the management of the Allied Terrier Club Show at the Royal Aquarium in London, and in 1891 the first Crufts show was booked in to the Royal Agricultural Hall in Islington where there were an impressive 2,437 entries. The Kennel Club took over as organisers of Crufts in 1948 and the show was first televised in 1950. In 2000, the category of Rescue Dog Agility was introduced to the programme, giving rescue dogs their well-deserved moment in the spotlight. The Best in Show prize has been awarded for the past 83 years, with 41 different breeds winning the sought-after title.

DID YOU KNOW?

The very first organised Field Trial took place at Southill, Bedfordshire, in 1865. A sport that quickly attracted a keen following among country gentlemen, this was probably the forerunner of the dog agility classes that have become so popular.

CRUFTS BEST IN SHOW WINNERS SINCE 2005

2016 Devon – West Highland Terrier

2015 Knopa – Scottish Terrier

2014 Afterglow Maverick Sabre – Standard Poodle

2013 Soletrader Peek A Boo – Petit Basset Griffon Vendéen

2012 Zentarr Elizabeth – Lhasa Apso

2011 The Kentuckian – Retriever (Flat Coated)

2010 Hungargunn Bear It'n Mind – Hungarian Vizsla

2009 Efbe's Hidalgo At Goodspice – Sealyham Terrier

2008 Philippe Olivier – Giant Schnauzer

2007 Fabulous Willy – Tibetan Terrier

2006 Caitland Isle Take a Chance – Australian Shepherd

2005 Cracknor Cause Celebre – Norfolk Terrier

DID YOU KNOW?

The death of King George VI on 6 February 1952 threatened the possibility of the cancellation of Crufts. The show did go ahead, but two days later than originally scheduled.

WORLDWIDE WOOFER SHOWS

Crufts might be one of the most established and renowned dog shows in the world, but the World Dog Show is still considered by many as the pinnacle of the dog show schedule. Held annually in one of the member countries of the Fédération Cynologique Internationale (FCI), more than 100 judges from 31 countries congregate to judge the dogs.

Other countries around the world hold their own major dog shows, including breed specific shows. Fun dog shows – or Companion Dog Shows, to give them their correct name – are often found at the local fete or festival and are also universally popular, allowing family dogs and mutts to compete. At smaller shows in the UK, classes such as Dog with the Waggiest Tail and Prettiest Bitch are run alongside sack races and basic dog agility classes.

PREPARING TO SHOW YOUR DOG

Allow plenty of time to get to the show and to register your dog for the classes you wish to participate in.

Pack carefully; make sure to include grooming tools, dog treats and plenty of poo bags. A bowl and some water is essential and, if it is summertime, take a water-soaked towel in a cool bag in case your dog overheats and needs to lie down on a chilled surface.

When you register to compete you will be given a ring number. This needs to be worn in the ring, so take a pin with you in case the fastening on your number isn't secure.

Pay attention to the Ring Steward and listen carefully to any tannoy announcements.

Go to a few shows as a spectator before entering. That way, you'll know what is expected of you and your dog. Note how the judges look over the dogs and see if you can spot what they are looking for.

Enjoy it! Both you and your dog should find shows a pleasurable experience, but if you discover that it really doesn't suit you or your dog then don't push it. Showing is not for everyone. Whatever happens, remember to tell your dog that it is wonderful and that it will always be YOUR winner.

GO FLYING

Flyball is a fast-paced competition that will see your dog burning off energy and having a ball at the same time. In this sport, two teams of four dogs compete at the same time, each using a parallel racing lane to run down. Dogs must clear four hurdles in succession before triggering a pedal on the Flyball box, thus releasing a tennis ball. The dog must catch and hold the ball before returning over the hurdles to the start line. The first team to have all dogs complete the course is declared the winner.

If you think your dog would enjoy and be good at Flyball, investigate groups in your area or keep an eye out at dog shows where Flyball teams often appear as a demonstration event.

DID YOU KNOW?

In the USA there are annual Crazy Dog Grooming contests. Entries include dogs with dyed fur and dogs dressed up as characters such Elvis or *Star Wars*' Yoda. The most bonkers designs can win dog owners up to $5,000 in prize money.

WHAT'S YOURS CALLED?

Registering a dog's show name is straightforward and can be done online at The Kennel Club's website. The Kennel Club's registration system records your puppy's birth and gives you the opportunity to give it a 'formal' name. It doesn't matter that you call it Rover or Bouncer at home; in the pedigree show ring your dog will be billed as whatever mouthful you bestow on the poor beast. The register can be cross-referenced, so you can be sure that your show name is unique. If you want to compete at Crufts then your dog must be registered with The Kennel Club on the Breed Register. Dogs originating from other countries must have an Authority To Compete number before they are permitted to compete at any show, and dogs can start competing from six months of age.

By and large, people who enjoy teaching animals to roll over will find themselves happier with a dog.

BARBARA HOLLAND

RECORD-BREAKING DOGS AROUND THE WORLD

Tallest – Zeus, a Great Dane measured 111.8 cm (44 in) tall
Michigan, USA, 2011

Smallest – Milly, a Chihuahua measured 9.65 cm (3.8 in) tall
Dorado, Puerto Rico, 2013

Longest tail – Irish Wolfhound Keon's tail measured 76.8 cm (30.2 in) long
Calgary, Canada, 2013

Finder of the largest truffle – an anonymous man credited his dog with sniffing out the largest-ever recorded truffle in the Apennines woodlands
Savigno near Bologna, Italy, 2014

Most expensive sheepdog – Marchup Midge for £10,080 ($16,216)
Skipton, Yorkshire, UK, 2012

Fastest dog to retrieve a person from water – Jack, a vom Mühlrad, covered 25 m (82 ft) in 1 minute, 36.81 seconds
Kaarst, Germany, 2013

Most treats balanced on a dog's nose – Monkey appeared on *Guinness World Records Unleashed* with 26 treats balanced on his nose
USA, 2013

The most dogs skipping on the same rope – no fewer than 14 dogs of Uchida Geinousha's Super Wan Wan Circus skipped on a rope in a televised record attempt
Fuji, Shizuoka, Japan, 2013

Most tennis balls held in the mouth by a dog – Augie, a Golden Retriever, gathered up and held five tennis balls in his chops
Dallas, Texas, USA, 2003

The loudest bark – measuring 113.1 dB, Golden Retriever Charlie was recorded during a 'Bark in the Park' event
Adelaide, Australia, 2012

RECORD BREAKING BIRTHS

Being a record breaker must have been of small comfort to Tia, a Neapolitan Mastiff back in 2004. Producing 24 pups, the largest-ever recorded litter, on 29 November 2004 the big momma gave birth to nine females and 15 males. Born by caesarean section, sadly one was stillborn and three died in the first week. Another record was broken in December 2014 when Keeler the Dobermann surprised her owner Zara Hayes from Nottinghamshire, UK, by delivering a litter of 14 bundles of squirmy joy – a British record for a Dobermann litter – just in time for Christmas.

BIGGEST AND SMALLEST CANINE BUDDIES

When Digby the Chihuahua was brought into the Southbridge RSPCA centre in 2015 he immediately found a friend. Although he had to jump up onto a chair in order to be nose-to-nose with his new pal, he and Nero – a 58-kilogram (130-pound) Mastiff – quickly became inseparable. Looking like his small buddy's minder, and proving that his heart is as big as he is, Nero now keeps a watchful eye on the poor little pup, who was found hiding behind bins in north London.

MOST UNLIKELY CANINE BUDDIES

There have been many reports of unlikely friendships springing up between dogs and other members of the animal kingdom. Dogs have befriended elephants, orangutans, lion cubs and even, as is the case with Roo and Penny, chickens. Roo the two-legged Chihuahua from Georgia, USA, was only seven weeks old when he was found abandoned in a park. His front legs were not properly developed and so a wheelchair was designed and fitted to the pup to enable him to get about. His best friend, Penny, just happens to be a chicken. Just nine weeks old when Alicia Williams saved her from a laboratory, Penny is a Silky, a breed well known for its fine and soft feathers. The two immediately struck up a firm, if unusual, friendship – one that has turned them into an internet sensation.

The dog lives for the
day, the hour, even
the moment.

ROBERT FALCON SCOTT

WORK LIKE A DOG

* * * * * * * * * * * *

[They] bark when there is a stranger about, but it is an expression of unmitigated joy at the chance to meet somebody...

NORMAN STRUNG ON HOW LABRADORS MAKE VERY FRIENDLY WATCHDOGS

* * * * * * * * * * * *

MAN'S BEST FRIEND

Dogs have worked with and for man for centuries in a wide variety of roles. Using strength, stamina, intelligence and, of course, their incredible sense of smell, their natural talents have been – and continue to be – well utilised.

DID YOU KNOW?

Shepherds and farmers have used dogs for many years to herd sheep, cattle and other animals. The practice inspired a television show, *One Man and His Dog*, in which sheepdogs competed. The show ran for 23 years on the BBC until 2013, when it was incorporated into *Countryfile*.

FRIENDS, ROMANS...

Our canine friends have long been used as workers. In domestic service 'turnspit dogs' were used to turn a treadmill that was linked to a roasting spit or to a butter-churning can, while the ancient Greeks used to breed a Mastiff-like dog, which they used as a highly efficient protection officer. The Greeks also bred a hound dog for hunting hares, which they trained to track the quarry and drive it into traps. The Romans used Mastiffs in their gladiatorial shows and called their breed Molossus. An aggressive fighting dog, it came as some surprise to the Romans when, on arrival in England, they discovered that the English Mastiff was even bigger and fiercer than theirs. The Romans also employed dogs to hunt and to guard homes and livestock.

PRAYER PUPS AND
HARD HOUNDS

When the barbarians invaded the Roman Empire they brought with them dogs such as the Tibetan prayer dog (now better known as the Tibetan Spaniel). They were trained to turn the prayer wheel in monasteries, in which monks would place prayers written on parchments. The theory was that, as the wheel revolved, the prayers were being constantly 'said'. A lesser-known job of these dogs was as hand-warmers. The monks would sit on the floor with their legs crossed and their hands folded inside the sleeves of their robes, and inside the sleeve nestled a cosy little dog!

When an eighty-five
pound mammal licks
your tears away, then
tries to sit on your lap,
it's hard to feel sad.

KRISTAN HIGGINS

DOG SLOG

In more modern times dogs have been, and continue to be, used in therapy by people suffering from depression, anger management issues or chronic illnesses. In clinical settings dogs are used to comfort the terminally ill, and also as assistants they provide invaluable support to those with impaired sight, hearing and mobility. Employed in farming, sled pulling, rescue missions, in warfare, policing and on country estates (by retrieving fowl and fish) man's best friend is no shirker when it comes to hard work.

A dog has one aim
in life... to bestow
his heart.

J. R. ACKERLEY

A NOSE FOR IT

A dog has an incredible sense of smell and taste, with some breeds boasting 'super snouts' that are invaluable in police work for locating drugs. A dog's senses can also provide support in healthcare, and the charity Medical Detection Dogs works with researchers, NHS trusts and universities to help train dogs to recognise the odours of human diseases such as cancer and diabetes. Another charity, Support Dogs, trains dogs to assist those suffering with epilepsy, the most common neurological illness. Seizure alert dogs are trained to provide a 100 per cent reliable warning up to 50 minutes prior to a seizure occurring, giving their owners time to find a place of safety and privacy before the seizure strikes.

Everything I know,
I learned from dogs.

NORA ROBERTS

KONNIE'S NOSE FOR TROUBLE

Konrad (Konnie to his loving family), a Standard Poodle, had a talent for sniffing out problems. Owner Kate recalls:

> The first time we noticed his gift was when my daughter had had a C-section. She had been home from hospital for about a week when one morning Konnie walked up to her chair and pushed his nose into her lap. He kept doing this all day, which had us rattled as it was totally out of character. By the evening he was really shoving his nose at my daughter's 'nether regions' and at the same time she began to feel unwell. A few hours later her temperature was seriously raised and the doctor ordered an ambulance. It was discovered that she had developed an internal infection as a result of her caesarean.

We put Konnie's behaviour down to coincidence but then a month later he started hassling our elderly Pug cross bitch. She had been spayed and Konnie had never troubled her before, but now he kept nudging her rear end. One day she rolled on to her back and to my horror there was a large swelling. It turned out to be a mammary tumour and it was removed. Konnie didn't bother her again until some months later. When he started again, this time I looked and the tumour was back!

Another time he followed a dog in the forest. I asked the owner if the dog was OK then she said the dog had just been diagnosed with diabetes. Then there was a three-legged greyhound who had lost her leg after a hit and run. Konnie started sniffing her amputation site so I asked her owner if she was OK. She said she was but got her checked out anyway – and lo and behold the dog had an infection.

DID YOU KNOW?

Used by monks to help find lost or stranded travellers in the Alps, St Bernard dogs were originally called 'hospice dogs' because they assisted at the Great St Bernard Hospice. Over time, however, they became known by the name of the hospice itself.

DID YOU KNOW?

An early suggestion of guide dogs is depicted in art. Uncovering a mural buried amid the ruins of ancient Herculaneum, Italy, archaeologists saw featured in the picture a dog clearly leading a blind man.

DISABILITY DOGS

The UK charity, Canine Partners, does incredible work training dogs to act as the limbs of disabled people. Founded in 1990 by dog welfare campaigner Anne Conway and vet Liz Ormerod, Canine Partners is the result of research into assistance dog programmes around the world. Based on the model of The SOHO Foundation of Holland – an established assistance dog's programme – and with similar organisations elsewhere in the world, dogs are trained to do everything from picking up dropped items to unloading washing machines. Dogs can also help their owners to get undressed, open doors and to hand money or cards to cashiers in shops. Obviously 'cleaning up' after a dog when you are out and about is not an option for a disabled person, so all Canine Partner dogs are trained to go to the toilet on command, enabling the disabled person to establish a designated dog loo area in his or her own garden. From soldiers who have lost the use of their limbs in war to those with long-term disabilities, a Canine Partner dog can transform the quality of a person's life.

GUIDE DOGS

The first organised attempt to train guide dogs was at a hospital for the blind in Paris in 1780. In 1788, Josef Reisinger, a blind sieve-maker from Vienna, trained a Spitz so effectively that people sometimes questioned whether he was genuinely blind.

Modern guide dogs date back to World War One, when numerous soldiers returned from the front blinded, often by poison gas. A German doctor, Dr Gerhard Stalling opened the world's first guide dog school for the blind in Oldenburg in 1916.

In the 1920s, American Dorothy Harrison Eustis began training dogs for the army, police and customs service in Switzerland, and it was Eustis who launched the guide dog movement internationally. Setting up guide dog schools in Switzerland and the USA, she named the schools The Seeing Eye. In 1930, after hearing about The Seeing Eye, two British women, Muriel Crooke and Rosamund Bond, contacted Eustis, who dispatched one of her trainers to the UK. In 1934 the two British women founded The Guide Dogs for the Blind Association. Since then guide dog schools have opened all around the world.

When you and your
beloved dog rely on
each other for nearly
everything, your love
is multiplied to
epic proportions.

DIANNE PHELPS, UNSIGHTED, WHO
HAS HAD SEVEN GUIDE DOGS

HEARING DOGS

Dogs can also be trained to alert deaf people to various sounds and danger signals, and in so doing provide a life-changing level of independence, confidence and companionship. The charity Hearing Dogs for Deaf People came about after Professor Lee Bustad, Dean of the School of Veterinary Medicine at Washington State University, included reference to the training of dogs to assist deaf people in the USA in a speech he gave at the British Small Animal Veterinary Association International Symposium in 1979. Dr Bruce Fogle, a vet present at the conference, was immediately interested in learning more. He contacted the Royal National Institute for the Deaf (now named Action on Hearing Loss) and in 1981 Fogle and Lady Wright from the National Institute succeeded in piloting a scheme in the UK. The scheme was officially launched in February 1982 at Crufts in London.

AN 'OUT OF THIS WORLD' MONGREL

Stray mongrels have been used in all sorts of horrible experiments in the past, and sadly, in some quarters, they still are today. In 1957, a stray mongrel called Laika was selected by scientists in the Soviet Union who wanted to conduct a very particular experiment: to confirm their belief that organisms from Earth could survive in space.

To prove their theory they sent the world's second artificial space satellite, *Sputnik 2*, into space with Laika on board. Attached to a life-support system, it was reported that Laika suffered no ill effects, even at an altitude of 3,200 kilometres (2,000 miles), but then, tragically, her life-support system ran out of batteries just a couple of days into her incredible journey. However, a report in 2002 suggested that she died from overheating and panic only hours after the mission began. The new evidence was presented at a World Space Congress in Houston, Texas, USA, by Dimitri Malashenkov of the Institute for Biological Problems in Moscow.

A monument honouring fallen cosmonauts was erected in 1997 at Star City on the outskirts of Moscow. Laika, quite rightly, is featured with her fellow space travellers.

HOT SPOTS

English aristocrats during the early 1700s were among the first known to use Dalmatians to accompany their carriages. Dalmatians often ran in pairs, one on either side of the coach, offering an effective deterrent to highwaymen and conferring something of a social status. Later, these speedy spotty dogs were employed by firefighters. Happy to run with horses when a fire alarm rang, the Dalmatians would bark to alert those nearby that the fire wagon was about to come out of the fire station. Running alongside the horse-drawn vehicle, the dogs stood guard over the wagon, horses and firefighter's belongings while the fire was dealt with. Many stations in the USA and the UK adopted the Dalmatian as a mascot even when vehicles were no longer horse drawn, keeping one in residence to see off rats and mice. Today the Dalmatian remains the breed that is associated with fire services.

During World War One, dogs were used to locate the wounded on the battlefield and today, dogs are trained to find and rescue people in disaster situations, such as earthquakes and floods, saving lives that otherwise would almost certainly be lost.

DOGS IN SPORT

I see you stand like
greyhounds in the slips,
Straining upon the start.
The game's afoot:
Follow your spirit; and
upon this charge,
Cry 'God for Harry! England!
and Saint George!

SHAKESPEARE, *HENRY V*

SPEEDY HOUNDS

Greyhounds and Huskies are known for their speed and strength, while scent following is becoming increasingly popular as a competitive sport for dogs of all breeds.

DID YOU KNOW?

To curtail foul play, in 1928 rules for racing were dictated through the newly founded National Greyhound Racing Club. Vets were required to check that dogs were fit to race and had not been doped or nobbled in any way, and the organisation updated the rules annually. All tracks and individuals had to be licensed by the club, and by 1928 all dogs had to have passports or identity books. These rules are still used today.

GREYHOUND RACING

Just as horse racing divides opinion, with some believing it to be cruel, the same applies to the racing of Greyhounds. Certainly in its early days the sport left a great deal to be desired in terms of the dogs' welfare, but there have been significant strides of improvement since then. The Greyhound Board of Great Britain now spends approximately one third of its annual budget on welfare – in excess of £4,000,000 – investing in aspects of racing including track safety, kennel conditions and the welfare of retired Greyhounds. The GBGB also works closely with major welfare charities via the Greyhound Knowledge Forum. Representatives include the RSPCA, Blue Cross and Dogs Trust. And whether you love or loathe Greyhound racing (and if it's the latter then there are certainly organisations that lobby against it that you can add your voice to), what cannot be ignored is the rich history of Greyhound racing and some of its incredible champions.

THE START OF THE RACE

A sport enjoyed by many, Greyhound racing as we know it today was brought to Britain by American Owen Patrick Smith. Smith was the inventor of the mechanical lure that could be run on an oval track, rather than the straight track which had been used previously. Immediately seeing the potential for international appeal, Smith and his colleagues set up the Greyhound Racing Association (GRA) and promptly built and opened the Belle Vue Stadium in Gorton, Manchester, in 1926. At the inaugural meeting in July of that year, 1,700 people watched six races. Word of mouth was positive, and before long numbers swelled and crowds of 11,000 were attending meetings.

Stadiums across the country began springing up, with London's White City, originally built for the 1908 Olympic Games, turned into a Greyhound racetrack. In 1927 White City hosted the first English Greyhound Derby, offering a staggering prize of £1,000. The Derby remains the highlight of the Greyhound racing calendar. In 2017, it will be held for the first time at Towcester Greyhound Stadium.

Today there are 25 tracks in England and Scotland, with the sport still attracting racegoers of all ages.

You may know a gentleman by his horse, his hawk and his greyhound.

OLD WELSH PROVERB

A SPEEDY STUD

A Greyhound that smashed a Sydney track record to win its first race was retired to stud because he could earn more money off the track. In April 2014 Shakey Jakey took a phenomenal 22-length lead to win the sixth race at Sydney's Wentworth Park. An offer of AUS$700,000 was made to owner David Pringle, topped by a second offer of AUS$1,000,000, but canny Pringle refused both. Instead he decided to retire Shakey Jakey to stud, which has since seen him amassing a fortune in stud fees.

MUSH! THE BEGINNINGS OF SLED RACING

Sled dogs have been 'on the pull' for some 4,000 years. As well as needing dogs for protection and hunting, people in the frozen north depended on dogs for transport. Great explorers like Amundsen, Peary and Byrd would never have made it to the icy wildernesses of the polar regions without sled dogs, and they have also played a key part in the civilisation of the world's snowbound zones. These splendid creatures also assisted in both world wars and, by 1873, were working with the Canadian Mounties.

DID YOU KNOW?

In 1925, doctors realised that Nome, Alaska, was on the brink of a diphtheria epidemic, and that the only serum that could prevent it was in Washington, over 960 kilometres (600 miles) away. With the engine of the fastest aircraft frozen and unable to start, it fell to teams of Huskies to race from Anchorage to Nome to deliver the precious cargo. It was Balto the Siberian Husky that lead the team of Huskies on the final leg of the journey. A statue of him now stands in New York's Central Park to commemorate the Nome serum run and bears the inscription 'Endurance, Fidelity, Intelligence'. The Iditarod Trail Race was launched in the 1970s and is held annually in March in memory of the great journey.

I am as confounded
by dogs as I am
indebted to them.

ROGER CARAS

THE RACE IS ON!

Starting from Winnipeg, Manitoba, and finishing in St Paul, Minnesota, the first established sled dog race is recorded as having taken place in 1850 (although it is likely that informal racing was commonplace before then). Growing in popularity, sled dog racing now takes place all over the world – even in places where snow is as rare as purple-spotted Dalmatians.

If you live in the UK then the Siberian Husky Club of Great Britain is a great place to start if you're keen to find out more about competing or spectating. The club's Aviemore Sled Dog Rally is the longest running and largest event of its kind in the UK, which, while somewhat ambitious for a newcomer to the sport, attracts over 200 teams each year. It is suitable for all ages, and there is even a competition for juniors.

British sled dog races usually take place on a woodland or forest circuit. Teams start racing at timed intervals and are divided into classes based on the number of dogs in the team.

SLED DOG RACE CLASSES

A – no more than eight dogs, no less than five

B – no more than six dogs, no less than four

C – no more than four dogs, no less than three

D – two dogs only

E – no more than three dogs, no less than two

U – unlimited, no less than five dogs

Junior 1 – one dog (dog one year+ / driver aged 12–15)

Junior 2 – one to two dogs (dog one year+/ driver aged 8–11)

Cani-Cross – one dog and a competitor, racing on foot

Bike-Joring – one dog and a driver pedalling on a bicycle

Scooter 1 – one dog and a driver riding a two-wheeled scooter

DID YOU KNOW?

The Disney film *Iron Will* features the 1917 version of the Winnipeg to St Paul race, which was won by Albert Campbell, a Métis from Pas, Manitoba.

DID YOU KNOW?

In Australia tracking is a popular recreational sport for many dogs and their owners. All types of dogs complete in tracking trials, from toy breeds to larger dogs like Rottweilers.

SCENT TRACKING

A dog sport that sees dogs picking up on a scent and following it across a terrain to an ultimate target, scent tracking is gaining popularity all over the world. A defined track has a starting point in an open space, and is a fun element of training that is usually given to help dogs become search or search-and-rescue workers.

The dogs are given a scent to follow from a person who has walked the course before the dogs arrive. The competing dogs then race, often over obstacles such as fences, hills and streams, to locate an object or target at the end of the track. Information on tracking trials in your local area should be available from local dog-focused organisations and from national bodies such as The Kennel Club.

DOGS
IN ART

•᛫᛫᛫᛫᛫᛫᛫᛫᛫᛫•

If you eliminate smoking and gambling, you will be amazed to find that almost all an Englishman's pleasures can be, and mostly are, shared by his dog.

GEORGE BERNARD SHAW

•᛫᛫᛫᛫᛫᛫᛫᛫᛫᛫•

CANINE-INSPIRED PAINTING

The favourite subject of many famous artists down the ages, dogs feature in critically acclaimed art in galleries all over the world. From American artist Cassius Marcellus Coolidge's famous *Dogs Playing Poker* series, to Édouard Manet's *A King Charles Spaniel* – one in a series of dog portraits by the Impressionist – canine-inspired painting is a trend that has endured.

On greetings cards, jigsaw puzzles, place mats, calendars and in advertising too, dogs remain a hugely popular image. Indeed, the *Dogs Playing Poker* series was created when Coolidge was commissioned to come up with an advertising campaign for cigars. Two of these paintings later sold for just under $6,000,000. You could say that this was 'a pair' that saw the artist enjoying a 'straight flush' in terms of success.

DID YOU KNOW?

The Kennel Club Dog Art Gallery in London houses the largest collection of dog paintings in Europe. It is open Monday to Friday by appointment.

DID YOU KNOW?

Touring Japan in 1937, Helen Keller, author, activist and the first deaf–blind person to earn a bachelor's degree, was given an Akita, which she asked for having heard the story of Hachikō.

ANDO'S HACHIKŌ

A sculpture of an Akita called *Hachikō*, by Japanese sculptor Takeshi Ando, stands in Tokyo's Shibuya train station. In the 1920s Hachikō would see his master off to work at the station every morning, returning to collect him at the end of the day. When his owner died in 1925 Hachikō refused to leave the station, waiting in vain for his master to come home. Regular passengers soon realised what was happening and they began to bring food for Hachikō. News of the dog's incredible loyalty spread far and wide and, in 1934, the statue of Hachikō was erected at the station, where by that time the dog had been waiting for his master for almost ten years. When Hachikō died in 1935, his bones were laid to rest next to his master's grave. With the outbreak of World War Two and metal being a precious commodity, Hachikō's statue was melted down in order to make arms. However, after the war a group of Hachikō's fans had another statue commissioned. Erected in 1948, the new memorial to this loyal Akita stands proudly to this day.

BOBBY AND CANEM

Other notable statues of dogs include a memorial to the dog known as Greyfriars Bobby. In 1858 John Gray was buried in Greyfriars Kirkyard in Edinburgh, Scotland. His dog Bobby, a Skye Terrier, is said to have slept on his master's grave for the following 14 years until his own death – a tale of such loyalty that a statue was the least the little dog deserved.

Meanwhile the Canary Islands proudly display a statue of the rare breed of dog, called *Canem* in Latin, after which the islands are named. Cast in bronze and lolling on a plinth in Las Palmas, the dog reminds people that the Canaries are in fact named after dogs rather than birds.

My dogs have been my most loyal friends and constant companions.

CESAR MILLAN

DID YOU KNOW?

Many portraits in the Royal Collection, which is held in trust for the UK by Queen Elizabeth II, depict dogs and their regal owners, with some pets even captured on canvas or sculpted alone. After his death, a life-size marble statue of Noble, Queen Victoria's beloved Collie, was sculpted by Princess Louise, Queen Victoria's daughter, and now stands in Osborne House on the Isle of Wight.

The dog alone,
of all brute animals,
has... an affection
upwards to man.

SAMUEL TAYLOR COLERIDGE

OLD MASTERS

Artist Pierre-Auguste Renoir often featured small dogs in his works. These include *Madame Renoir with a Dog*, which was painted in 1880. Another famous painting that includes a canine subject is *Portrait of Giovanni Arnolfini and his Wife*, also known as *The Arnolfini Portrait*. Painted by Netherlandish artist Jan van Eyck and hanging in London's National Gallery, the scene is of a wedding between an Italian merchant and a colleague's daughter. At their feet is a small Terrier. The dog is said to symbolise fidelity, companionship and love. If you look carefully you can also see the artist in the picture – he included himself in the background reflected in the mirror as a painter creating the subject's portrait.

PICASSO'S LUMP

Pablo Picasso was born in Spain in 1881 and is believed by many to be the greatest and most influential artist of the twentieth century. A painter, sculptor, printmaker, ceramicist and theatrical set designer, he was also the co-founder of the Cubist movement, as well as a pioneer of several other styles. He was also devoted to his dog, a Dachshund called Lump. Originally belonging to photographer David Douglas Duncan, when the pooch met Picasso in 1957 the match was one made in heaven. Allowing Lump access all areas, including his studio, the great artist featured his beloved dog in more than 15 of his works. Master and dog died within weeks of each other after a partnership of 16 years.

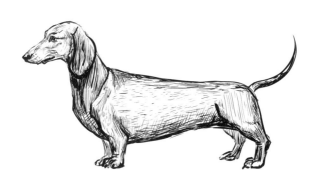

Whosoever loveth me,
loveth my hound.

THOMAS MORE

DID YOU KNOW?

During the Renaissance, detailed portraits of the dog as a symbol of fidelity and loyalty appeared in mythological, allegorical and religious art throughout Europe and could be found on the easels of Jan van Eyck, Leonardo da Vinci, Albrecht Dürer and Diego Velázquez.

DID YOU KNOW?

Dogs were regularly featured in Greek art. Famous subjects include Cerberus, the three-headed hound guarding the entrance to hell, and the hunting dogs that accompanied the virgin goddess of the chase, Diana.

WHAT THE DICKENS?!

Having adopted a rescue dog, photographer Dan Bannino was inspired to embark on an artistic project that entailed using models from a local dog shelter. *Poetic Dogs* entailed four months-worth of work at the shelter learning about his subjects and trying to figure out how to transform the dogs into his favourite authors. Untrained, fearful and completely inexperienced as models, Bannino had to ditch his camera flash and stuff his pockets full of dog treats in order to secure canine cooperation. Costuming the dogs came next, and then much waiting around whilst being poised to snap the exact expressions he needed. The incredible photographs, including canine equivalents of Charles Dickens, Peggy Guggenheim, Ernest Hemingway, Leo Tolstoy and Mark Twain, can be viewed online.

DOGS IN LITERATURE

Toto did not really care whether he was in Kansas or the Land of Oz so long as Dorothy was with him.

L. FRANK BAUM

LITERARY STARS

Bullseye in *Oliver Twist*, Pilot in *Jane Eyre*, Scamper in *The Secret Seven* and a whole host of canine characters in the novels of Jilly Cooper – dogs are often featured in books and are sometimes integral to the plot. As for poetry, their antics and characters have been well used as subject matter.

> Tom told his dog called Tim to beg,
> And up at once he sat,
> His two clear amber eyes fixed fast,
> His haunches on his mat. Tom poised
> a lump of sugar on
> His nose; then, 'Trust!' says he;
> Stiff as a guardsman sat his Tim;
> Never a hair stirred he.
>
> 'Paid for!' says Tom; and in a trice
> Up jerked that moist black nose;
> A snap of teeth, a crunch, a munch,
> And down the sugar goes!

Walter de la Mare, 'Tom's Little Dog'

Did you know that there are over three hundred words for love in canine?

GABRIELLE ZEVIN

WHERE IT BEGAN

Often cast in great works of literature and in popular books today, dogs have inspired novelists, playwrights and poets for thousands of years. It is believed that the first author of canine literature was a Roman scholar called Marcus Terentius Varro (116–27 BCE). A philosopher who wrote extensively on many different subjects, including agriculture, in his work *Rerum rusticarum libri tres (Three Books on Agriculture)* he proffers advice on different breeds, the canine diet and even gives pointers on training.

DID YOU KNOW?

In the King James Bible, dogs are mentioned on 14 occasions. The only dog mentioned by specific breed is the Greyhound, which occurs in Proverbs 30:29–31.

There be three things which go well,
yea, four are comely in going:
A lion, which is strongest among beasts,
and turneth not away for any;
A greyhound; an he-goat also; and a king...

FAMOUS CHARACTERS

Dogs were given starring roles in early fables such as Aesop's *The Dog and the Shadow*, from which the reader learns that being greedy and clutching at shadows is not a sensible way of conducting oneself. Shakespeare also makes mention of dogs, although it is only in *The Two Gentlemen of Verona* that a dog gets anything approaching a decent role (the cheeky mongrel, Crab, who belongs to the servant Launce). Some other breeds that do at least get a shout-out from the Bard include Greyhounds (*Henry V*); Spaniels (*Antony and Cleopatra*); Greyhounds, mongrels and Spaniels (*Macbeth*); and Hounds (*A Midsummer Night's Dream*).

In the past 200 years we have also seen dogs cropping up in the works of great writers like Charles Dickens. Who can fail to feel at least a degree of pity for the poor terrier, Bullseye, the dog belonging to bully-boy Bill Sikes in *Oliver Twist*? Treated appallingly by Sikes, Dickens describes the dog as vicious and keeps him loyal to Bill and his aggressive, thieving ways right to the bitter end. It suggests that perhaps the great writer knew something of the loyalty of a canine friend.

... a great dog, whose black and white colour made him a distinct object against the trees... a lion-like creature with long hair and a huge head...

JANE EYRE, ON MEETING PILOT, MR ROCHESTER'S DOG, FOR THE FIRST TIME IN *JANE EYRE* BY CHARLOTTE BRONTË

DOGS IN THE NURSERY

Dogs are frequently used as characters in children's literature, and one of the most famous is Nana the dog, the Newfoundland belonging to the Darling family in *Peter Pan* by J. M. Barrie. Said to have been inspired by Barrie's own dog, Nana howled her shaggy head off in a bid to alert the Darling parents that their children were absconding with Peter. In the book, Mr Darling is so mortified that he has ignored their faithful friend's warning siren that he takes it upon himself to sleep in her kennel in her place until his children are safely returned. Enid Blyton's *The Famous Five* and *The Secret Seven* books also include dogs; inevitably, Timmy and Scamper each play their parts in bringing down criminals and baddies.

DID YOU KNOW?

The term 'dog days of summer' was coined by the ancient Greeks and Romans and has endured to this day. For the ancients, the term referred to the rising of the 'Dog Star', Sirius, which coincided with the hottest days of summer.

TEN CHILDREN'S BOOKS
STARRING DOGS

1. *Clifford the Big Red Dog* by Norman Bridwell
2. *Dip the Puppy* by Spike Milligan
3. *Hairy Maclary from Donaldson's Dairy* by Lynley Dodd
4. The *Harry Potter* series (in which Fang and Fluffy, Hagrid's dogs appear) by J. K. Rowling
5. *Kipper the Dog* series by Mick Inkpen
6. *Spot the Dog* series by Eric Hill
7. *The Hundred and One Dalmatians* by Dodie Smith
8. *The Tale of Samuel Whiskers or The Roly-Poly Pudding* (John Joiner is the Terrier that foils the rats' plan to turn Tom Kitten into a pudding) by Beatrix Potter
9. *The Wizard of Oz* (Toto is Dorothy's faithful companion) by L. Frank Baum
10. *Walter the Farting Dog* by William Kotzwinkle and Glenn Murray

VERY CURIOUS

The investigation into the murder of Wellington, a Poodle, by a young autistic teenager seems perhaps an unlikely premise for a bestseller. But *The Curious Incident of the Dog in the Night-Time* by Mark Haddon was a smash hit, not just as a book but also as a stage adaptation which now plays to packed houses in London's West End and on Broadway.

FIDOS OF CONTEMPORARY FICTION

Cyril, Angus's dog with the gold tooth and a taste for beer, appears in Alexander McCall Smith's *44 Scotland Street* series, while in Jilly Cooper's Rutshire-based books, dogs get significant roles and fabulous names. But arguably the most famous doggy story of all time is Sheila Burnford's 1961 novel, *The Incredible Journey*. Later given the Disney treatment in 1963, this is the tear-jerking story of a Labrador, a Bull Terrier and a Siamese cat stranded hundreds of kilometres from home. Determined to make the journey across the Canadian wilderness and back to the bosom of their family, this glorious tale of courage and determination is a literary tribute to qualities of intelligence, loyalty, tenacity and resourcefulness – qualities that dogs have become associated with.

TEN DOGS AND THEIR LITERARY OWNERS

Quinine (Dachshund) and Anton Chekhov
Wessex (Terrier) and Thomas Hardy
Boatswain (Newfoundland) and Lord Byron
Cliché (Poodle) and Dorothy Parker
Bluebell (Greyhound) and Jilly Cooper
Chopper (Jack Russell) and Roald Dahl
Peter (Wire-haired Terrier) and Agatha Christie
Charley (Poodle) and John Steinbeck
Pongo (Pug) and Donna Tartt
Sapphire (Greyhound) and J. K. Rowling

ROVERS OF RHYME

Poetry about dogs has delighted us for generations. In anthologies all over the world you will find poems about different breeds, pet dogs, fierce dogs and even lyrical prayers for deceased dogs.

All in the town were still asleep,
When the sun came up with a shout and a leap.
In the lonely streets unseen by man,
A little dog danced. And the day began.

Rupert Brooke, from 'The Little Dog's Day'

One of the most famous pup poems is Elizabeth Barrett Browning's 'To Flush, My Dog'. A leading and prolific poet of the Victorian age, Browning is said to have loved Flush dearly and taken great comfort in his presence during her long-term poor health.

And if one or two quick tears
Dropped upon his glossy ears,
Or a sigh came double, –
Up he sprang in eager haste,
Fawning, fondling, breathing fast,
In a tender trouble.

And this dog was satisfied,
If a pale thin hand would glide,
Down his dewlaps sloping, –
Which he pushed his nose within,
After, – platforming his chin
On the palm left open.

Elizabeth Barrett Browning, from 'To Flush, My Dog'

FRIEND OR FOE?

Hark! hark! the dogs do bark,
The beggars are coming to town.
Some in rags, and some in tags,
And some in velvet gowns.

Dating back to thirteenth-century England, this rhyme explains how communities used dogs to warn them that strangers were approaching. During this period of history, beggars and minstrels travelled around and often included coded messages of rebellion in their performances and recitals. Passing gossip and propaganda to the common people in lyrics and rhymes led to devious plots and uprisings against those in power, and so all incoming visitors were regarded with suspicion even if they were wearing 'velvet gowns'.

DOGS IN MUSIC

When there are dogs
and music, people
have a good time.

EMMYLOU HARRIS

POP DOGS

As with art and literature, dogs have moved musicians and lyricists to write and record songs that pay homage to man and woman's best friend. In one instance a dog-loving super-group even recorded a secret message for dogs on one of their album tracks. Sir Paul McCartney has admitted that on The Beatles' *Sgt. Pepper's Lonely Hearts Club Band* album recorded in 1967, they included a recording of an ultrasonic whistle, a sound that only dogs can hear. The whistle is included in the track 'A Day in the Life' – dig out your copy and give your hound a musical message.

HOW MUCH OF A HIT?

A popular novelty song that has endured is '(How Much is) That Doggie in the Window?' Written by Bob Merrill in 1952, the original version was recorded in the USA by Patti Page and released in January 1953 by Mercury Records. It reached number one on both the *Billboard* and *Cash Box* magazine charts and sold in excess of two million copies. Lita Roza, was the first British female to go to number one in the hit parade with a cover of the song. The song entered the charts in March 1953 at number nine and then spent 11 weeks in the charts, reaching number one in April. It was also the first number one with a question in its title!

DID YOU KNOW?

In 2013, a woman reported sleepless nights over a three-year period after being beleaguered by a rare illness involving the song '(How Much is) That Doggie in the Window?' According to a report in *The Telegraph* newspaper, Susan Root suffered from a form of tinnitus where music and songs played endlessly in her head, day and night. Susan's favourite childhood song has been stuck in her head since 2010.

CLASSICAL CANINES

Does your dog chill out to Chopin or relax to Ravel? A 2014 study revealed that classical music might be the most effective way of calming a dog that is displaying anxious or fearful behaviour. Led by Dr Lori R. Kogan of Colorado State University, the study found that mutts loved the music of Mozart and his classical chums so much that it appeared to reduce levels of stress in the dogs involved in the trial. Publishing her findings in the *Journal of Veterinary Behavior*, Kogan said that she concluded that classical music was more soothing than the specially made pet-calming CDs or any other genre of music.

No symphony orchestra
ever played music like a
two-year-old girl laughing
with a puppy.

BERN WILLIAMS

THE DOG ATE MY OPERA

When Richard Wagner was trying to finish his opera *Die Meistersinger von Nürnberg* his musical genius was tested by the constant whining of a dog. His landlord had tied up a Bulldog named Leo outside the front of the house – and Leo was clearly less than impressed with Wagner's music. Taking pity on the dog, the great composer called a servant to help him free Leo. Much good it did him though – the dog promptly bit Wagner on the thumb, triggering an infection. Unable to write for six months, his publisher was not best pleased and must surely have looked upon the excuse 'the dog bit my writing hand' with as much suspicion as the proverbial 'the dog ate my homework'.

DID YOU KNOW?

George Gershwin's *Walking the Dog* – intended to conjure up a jazzy saunter around Manhattan – has a delightful swinging rhythm and a perky clarinet solo. Written for the 1937 film *Shall We Dance*, the piece provided the accompaniment for a scene in which a dog is walked on a luxury liner.

THE POOCH HIT PARADE

Patti Page/Lita Roza – '(How Much is) That Doggie in the Window?' (1953)

Elvis Presley – 'Hound Dog' (1956)

Rufus Thomas – 'Walking the Dog' (1963)

Cat Stevens – 'I Love My Dog' (1966)

Johnny Cash – 'Dirty Old Egg-Sucking Dog' (1966)

The Stooges – 'I Wanna Be Your Dog' (1969)

Lobo – 'Me and You and a Dog Named Boo' (1971)

Led Zeppelin - 'Black Dog' (1971)

Donny Osmond – 'Puppy Love' (1972)

Nick Drake – 'Black Eyed Dog' (1974)

Brian and Michael – 'Matchstalk Men and Matchstalk Cats and Dogs' (1978)

George Clinton – 'Atomic Dog' (1982)

Kate Bush – 'Hounds of Love' (1985)

Pulp – 'Dogs are Everywhere' (1986)

Snoop Dogg (featuring Tha Dogg Pound) – 'Doggy Dogg World' (1993)

Baha Men – 'Who Let The Dogs Out?' (2000)

Florence + The Machine – 'Dog Days are Over' (2009)

'DADDY WOULDN'T BUY ME A BOW WOW'

A favourite of music halls of the time, in 1892 Joseph Tabrar wrote what was to become a traditional song that is still sung around camp fires, on long car journeys and in playschools today. It has even been performed by The Muppets!

I love my little cat, I do,
With soft black silky hair;
It comes with me each day to school,
And sits upon the chair;
When teacher says, 'Why do you bring
That little pet of yours?'
I tell her that I bring my cat
Along with me because –

Daddy wouldn't buy me a bow-wow, bow wow.
Daddy wouldn't buy me a bow-wow, bow wow.
I've got a little cat,
And I'm very fond of that.
But I'd rather have a bow wow,
wow, wow, wow, wow.

Joseph Tabrar, 'Daddy Wouldn't Buy Me a Bow Wow'

A HOWLING SUCCESS

Some dogs really do appear to 'sing'. In July 2014, Oakley the Australian Shepherd dog was filmed 'singing' along to the title song of the Disney blockbuster *Frozen*. Other dogs seem inspired to throw back their heads and howl like *The X Factor* contestants when they hear particular pieces of music. For Michelle O'Brien from Worthing, West Sussex, the song that set her mongrel Bertie off was Elvis Presley's *Jailhouse Rock*. Easy enough to avoid – or it would have been, but for the fact that Jim, her husband, was an Elvis impersonator. 'The song was one of the best in his repertoire,' explained O'Brien, 'but whenever he rehearsed it Bertie would join in and eventually I got fed up with the neighbours complaining and he had to drop it from his set. It was the only number that affected Bertie this way – he never even lifted his head from his paws when Jim did *Hound Dog*!'

There is no psychiatrist in the world like a puppy licking your face.

BERNARD WILLIAMS

DOGS IN ENTERTAINMENT

🐾 🐾 🐾 🐾 🐾 🐾 🐾 🐾 🐾

I was haunted by trainers going 'Up, up, up, get up'. You find yourself picking your head up and then realising, 'they aren't talking to me.'

JEFF DANIELS, ABOUT WORKING ON THE FILM *101 DALMATIANS*

🐾 🐾 🐾 🐾 🐾 🐾 🐾 🐾 🐾

DOGS IN THE SPOTLIGHT

Many dogs have found fame on the big and small screen, as well as on stage. From movie blockbusters to our favourite soap operas, our love of dogs is another sure-fire way for producers and programme makers to reel us in. Whether it's through cartoons, adaptations of books, sitcoms, their own series or even a titular role in a movie, the cute canine factor is not to be underestimated when it comes to matters financial. Making their mark from Hollywood to Broadway, from the West End to the BBC, dogs have entertained us since they began appearing in music halls and vaudeville.

EASTENDERS' TOP DOGS

Roly (Poodle) – belonging to the Watts family

Wellard (Tervuren Belgian Shepherd) – belonging to Robbie Jackson

'Little' Willy (Pug) – belonging to Ethel Skinner

Genghis (Irish Wolfhound) – belonging to the Miller family

Lady Di (Bulldog) – belonging to the Carter family

CORONATION STREET'S CUTEST CANINES

Eccles (Border Terrier) – most recently owned by the Barlow family

Schmeichel (Great Dane) – owned by Chesney Brown

Monica (Greyhound) – owned by Tyrone Dobbs

Ozzy (Black Labrador) – owned by Maria Connor

Rover (German Shepherd) – owned by Bet Lynch (previously Gilroy)

A dog can express more
with his tail in seconds
than his owner can
express with his
tongue in hours.

ANONYMOUS

WELL-KNOWN HOUNDS

Other famous soap dogs include Bouncer, a Golden Labrador, and also Audrey, the Cairn Terrier, both of whom were much adored in the Australian soap, *Neighbours*, while way back in the 1970s Benny in *Crossroads* had a little black and white mutt called Moses.

DID YOU KNOW?

Emmerdale had the honour of adding a very special trophy to its awards stash. Bracken, who played Edna's dog Batley, won Best Exit at the annual awards in 2002, making him the first soap animal to win a British Soap Award. Acting his paws off in the scenes when village vet Paddy diagnosed him with cancer, his ultimate demise left not a dry eye on the couches of the UK.

BLUE PETER'S PETRA

Britain's favourite kids' television show of the 1960s and 70s (and still going strong today), *Blue Peter* producers wanted to introduce a dog to the show so that young viewers who didn't have a pet could at least have a share in the programme's dog. Petra was the first *Blue Peter* dog, introduced in 1962. However, disaster struck when the mongrel died after just one appearance. Not wanting to upset thousands of children, a secret mission to find a lookalike began in earnest. One was discovered in a London pet shop, and Petra remained on the show until 1977, when she retired owing to ill health. News of her death later that year made national headlines. A statue to Petra stands in the *Blue Peter* garden.

Other *Blue Peter* dogs include: Patch, Shep, Goldie, Bonnie, Lucy, Mabel, Meg and Barney.

PUDSEY'S GOT TALENT

When dancing dog Pudsey appeared on television talent show *Britain's Got Talent* in 2012, he and his owner and trainer Ashleigh Butler became the act to beat. Ashleigh and Pudsey, a Border Collie–Bichon Frisé–Chinese Crested Powderpuff cross – won the hearts of first the nation and then the world – what's not to love about a young girl and a very cute dancing dog whose footwork is as nimble as any *Strictly Come Dancing* contestant's? A book deal, panto roles and *Pudsey the Dog: The Movie* followed, ensuring this clever little performer could keep himself in top-quality bones for the rest of his life.

ANIMATED AND ADORED

As for cartoon dogs, Snoopy – one of the most famous, especially in the USA – started as a comic strip. Brian Griffin, the dog in the outrageous adult cartoon *Family Guy* also has an enormous fan base, while Scooby-Doo is adored by generations. Other famous cartoon dogs include Dougal from *The Magic Roundabout*, Disney's Goofy and Pluto and, of course, *The Simpson's* dog, Santa's Little Helper. Gromit – the canine version of Jeeves in *Wallace and Gromit* – has won fans the world over as he rescues his hapless master from scrapes and disasters with a mix of calm, cunning and sheer resourcefulness.

EDDIE AND LONDON

Eddie the Jack Russell Terrier, real name Moose, received fan mail for his role in *Frasier*. The largest of his litter at birth, he went on to become even bigger in terms of his doggy status. *The Littlest Hobo* saw a dog called London, ironically a German Shepherd, having adventure after adventure as he wandered to a different place in each episode. Always helping those who were having a rough time, when his job was done London always trotted off, refusing to be adopted as a pet by those he had helped.

BATTERSEA'S WAIFS
AND STRAYS

English comedian and presenter Paul O'Grady has gifted London's Battersea Dogs Home the most incredible advertising campaign through his hugely popular television show, *For the Love of Dogs*.

Battersea and its satellite sites in Berkshire and Kent do incredible work in protecting and caring for dogs (and cats), and in 2015 Battersea cared for around 4,868 dogs.

It all began in 1860 with Mary Tealby, one determined dog lover who was extremely concerned about the huge number of animals roaming the streets of London. The home was originally called The Temporary Home for Lost and Starving Dogs. Located in Holloway, North London, the organisation moved to Battersea in 1871 and has been there ever since.

FROM DERELICT STABLES
TO BAFTA NOMINATION:
FASCINATING BATTERSEA FACTS

1860 – The Temporary Home for Lost & Starving Dogs is opened by Mrs Mary Tealby in disused stables in Holloway, North London

1862 – Charles Dickens writes an article supporting the Home's work in his newspaper, *All the Year Round*

1871 – The Home is relocated to Battersea

1885 – Queen Victoria becomes the Home's first Royal Patron

1914 – One hundred sled dogs are accommodated at one of the Home's other sites in readiness for Ernest Shackleton's second Antarctic Expedition

1956 – Queen Elizabeth II becomes the Home's patron

1984 – Prince Michael of Kent becomes President of the Home and the first full-time veterinary surgeon is employed

1990s – The Home pioneers the microchipping of dogs

2002 – The Home changes its name to Battersea Dogs & Cats Home

2012 – The first series of ITV's *Paul O'Grady: For the Love of Dogs* is screened to critical acclaim, scooping a National Television Award and a BAFTA nomination. The series attracted record viewing figures and, more importantly, highlighted the wonderful work of Battersea Dogs & Cats Home.

I have yet to see one completely unspoiled star, except for the animals - like Lassie.

EDITH HEAD

LEADING LADY LASSIE

Lassie Come Home was rewritten as a novel after first being published as a short story by Eric Knight in 1938. The book tells of a courageous Collie that bravely travelled hundreds of kilometres to return to her young owner. It quickly became a bestseller, and in 1941 Hollywood's MGM Studios bought the movie rights for $10,000 casting a dog named Pal and two human stars – a young Roddy McDowall and Elizabeth Taylor – in the central roles. The movie premiered in 1943, smashing box office records and delighting both critics and moviegoers alike. More films followed and, in 1947, the *Lassie* radio show launched, followed soon after by the television show. Running for 17 years, this award-winning show remains one of the longest running television programmes in history.

DID YOU KNOW?

Lassie merchandise from the films or television shows can be collector's items. *Lassie* collectors can be found all over the world, and the market is highly competitive.

TOP DOLLAR TOTO

Terry the Cairn Terrier that played Toto in the 1939 film *The Wizard of Oz* was a bitch and not, as the film claims, a male dog. An abandoned dog, Terry was rescued by Carl Spitz, a dog trainer. Landing her first film role in the 1934 romance, *Ready for Love*, Terry had a wonderfully successful career and was such a loveable dog that it is said Judy Garland begged to adopt her. Owner Carl Spitz refused, keeping Terry even when she retired from the movies. For her part as Toto in the original film of *The Wizard of Oz*, Terry was paid $125 a week – more than some of the film's human cast members.

DID YOU KNOW?

Nicknamed 'Rinty', Rin Tin Tin appeared in an impressive 27 Hollywood films and did a great public relations job for German Shepherds. In 1929 Rin Tin Tin received the most votes for the first Academy Award for Best Actor, but it was decided that the award should go to a human – a ruling that must surely have seen his hackles rise.

THE PLAY'S THE THING

On stage, some shows call for real dogs to appear. For the stage version of *Chitty Chitty Bang Bang* one scene calls for a pack of dogs to run across the stage on cue. Thanks to good training and plenty of rehearsals, this aspect of the production generally goes off without a hitch. However, anyone sitting close to the front with an open bag of sweets runs the risk of being mobbed by the show's canine cast.

When Andrew Lloyd Webber revived *The Wizard of Oz* for the London Palladium in 2011 he cast four Westies – all getting excellent reviews – to play the role of Toto.

In *Annie,* her beloved dog, Sandy, is a cast member that has sometimes given the young actress playing the title role a headache. One actress recalls playing the role at the Victoria Palace Theatre in London as a child:

At one point I was meant to call for Sandy and he would come bounding across the stage to me. Only sometimes he didn't and I'd be left in the middle of the stage practically pleading with the obstinate mutt to leave the wings and come to me. In the end I took to carrying a sausage in my pocket.

DID YOU KNOW?

Harry Potter dog, Fang, belonging to gamekeeper Hagrid, was played by three different Neapolitan Mastiffs in the films and was originally brought to life by male dog Hugo in *Harry Potter and the Philosopher's Stone*. In 2003, Hugo made a memorable television appearance with presenter Fern Britton, during which he drooled on her!

TOP FIVE HIGHEST GROSSING CANINE FILMS

1. *Scooby-Doo* (2002) $153,294,164 (cinemas only)
2. *Marley & Me* (2008) $143,153,751
3. *101 Dalmatians* (1996) $136,189,294
4. *Beverly Hills Chihuahua* (2008) $94,514,402
5. *Cats & Dogs* (2001) $93,385,515

COMMERCIAL CANINES

Many advertisers have used dogs to sell their wares. From insurance companies to toilet roll manufacturers, a cute woofer is a highly effective sales tool. Whether at the movies, online or at home, a clever, sweet-looking or funny dog is a sure-fire way of grabbing our attention – and advertisers know it. Big dogs like St Bernards send a subliminal message that suggests strength, while bouncy dogs like Labradors are used to promote products and services to a family audience.

DID YOU KNOW?

Billed as 'the patron saint of pipe smokers', the star of the St Bruno Pipe Tobacco adverts was, for many years, a vast but cuddly-looking St Bernard dog that always arrived with tobacco for the smoker who had run out.

PAINT, POOCHES

The furry mascot for Dulux paint became so well known that to many people it will always be a Dulux dog rather than an Old English Sheepdog. First appearing in the 1960s, this shaggy dog's story was told in 30 seconds: you too can transform your home with a lick of paint, as advertised by this gorgeous fur-ball. The first dog to be cast by Dulux was Shepton Dash, which remained the face of the brand for eight years. Shep was succeeded by Fernville Lord Digby. Both dogs were chauffeured to the studio and trained by famous dog trainer Barbara Woodhouse.

POLO AND PUP FOOD

Then there was the Volkswagon Polo dog. It was seen sitting in the car's passenger seat, being driven by a beautiful woman and belting out 'I'm a Man' by The Spencer Davis Group. The ad was dropped following complaints about suspected animal abuse but these proved to be completely untrue. Viewers who had suggested that the dog was trembling didn't realise that it was in fact standing on a motorised plate – a deliberate move to make it look as if it was trembling. In spite of the ad's huge popularity (more than 1,850,000 hits on YouTube), the ad remained dropped.

In 2012, Britain's first ever television advert specifically for dogs was created by Bakers, the dog food manufacturer. The ad included a high-frequency noise above 17,000 Hz, which can be heard only by dogs.

DID YOU KNOW?

Henry the Bloodhound starred with the late Sir Clement Freud, grandson of Sigmund Freud, in a dog food campaign in the 1960s. Both dog and actor shared the same gloomy expression – the reason a Bloodhound was selected.

HIS MASTER'S VOICE

Eventually becoming an iconic image of the twentieth century, Nipper the dog found fame through a record label. Pictured listening to a gramophone, the smooth-haired Fox Terrier became mascot, logo and trademark for the HMV brand. Painted by Francis Barraud, it wasn't until 1898, three years after Nipper's death, that Francis painted him in the world-famous pose. Entitling the painting *His Master's Voice*, the Royal Academy rejected it, which prompted him to patent the painting instead. He then offered the painting to The Gramophone Company Limited, who, in the early 1900s, changed their name to HMV after the painting. The rest is musical history.

BRAVE, INTELLIGENT AND LOYAL

The guard dog was incorruptible;
the police dog dependable; the
messenger dog reliable. The
human watchman might be
bought; not so the dog. The soldier
sentinel might fall asleep; never
the dog. The battlefield runner
might fail... but not the dog, to
his last breath would follow
the line of duty.

ERNEST HAROLD BAYNES

CANINE CADETS OF HISTORY

With bravery shown on the battlefield, in minefields and on patrol for the armed forces or police, there's no shortage of stories about the courage and intelligence of our four-legged friends.

Dogs in the army go back to the time of Christopher Columbus and his return to the Americas in 1495. Bringing dogs with him, he called them 'the most fearsome weapon of all'. During the American Revolutionary War, dogs were also used as sentry dogs. Guarding everything from groceries to guns to captives, the woofers raised the alarm when required to do so.

In World War One, dogs played many roles including finding bodies on the battlefield and identifying the wounded. The bigger dogs would drag the bodies of men to safety. They were also used to deliver messages to the front line, being faster and harder to aim at than a man. In 1918, thousands of dogs from The Battersea Dogs Home made up the first batch of recruits for the War Dog Training School. Trained to become messengers, sentries and munitions carriers, these extraordinary troops played a key role in the war.

THAT'S THE WAY TO
DO IT, JUDY

During World War Two, Judy, an English Pointer, served on a Royal Navy vessel where she was able to detect the sound of hostile aircraft far sooner than her fellow human crew members. Unfortunately, the vessel was a casualty of battle and sank, and the crew were captured and carted off to a prisoner-of-war camp. But resourceful Judy somehow wormed her way into the camp and helped her crew by bringing them scavenged scraps. Japanese guards tried several times to kill her, but Judy was too wily. After the war, RAF serviceman Frank Williams pestered the authorities to register Judy as an official prisoner of war, and she remains the only animal in history to be accorded this status.

DOGS OF WAR BY NUMBERS

145,000 – dogs cared for by four humans at The Battersea Home during World War Two

30,000 (approximately) – dogs employed by Germany in its war effort by 1918

20,000 (approximately) – dogs employed by Britain, France and Belgium in their war effort by 1918

One million – dogs died during World War One

$20,000 – the average bounty placed on the heads of military working dogs in the Vietnam War

10,000 – the estimated number of lives saved by dogs and handlers during the Vietnam War

5 per cent – dogs on the ground in Afghanistan and Iraq that suffered canine post-traumatic stress disorder and were treated with canine Prozac

Five – dogs are five times faster than the average soldier on foot

200,000+ – the number of domestic dogs slaughtered at the insistence of the UK Government during World War Two

One – the dog Hitler is reputed to have taken into the German trenches with him

LIAM AND THEO

When explosive search dog handler, Lance Corporal Liam Tasker, was paired with Theo, a Springer Spaniel cross, the two soon became inseparable. During a five-month stint in Afghanistan the pair saved countless lives, finding more bombs than any other soldier–dog pairing. But in February 2011, 26-year-old Liam was shot dead by the Taliban. Theo, who was not quite two years old and in great health, suffered a seizure and died just days later. Dying of a broken heart seems to be the only explanation for why this dog, as brave and true as his master, simply gave up on life.

DID YOU KNOW?

In World War One, Mercy Dogs were trained to carry medical supplies and find casualties on the battlefields. Soldiers who could tend to their own wounds helped themselves to the bandages and other first aid equipment, and for those who were so badly wounded that they were certain to die, there was some comfort in the presence of a Mercy Dog as they prepared for the end.

He is the one person to whom I can talk without the conversation coming back to war.

DWIGHT D. EISENHOWER
ON HIS SCOTTIE DOG

'FOR GALLANTRY' –
THE DICKIN MEDAL

A bronze medallion inscribed with the words 'For Gallantry' and 'We Also Serve', the Dickin Medal hangs on a green, dark brown and pale blue striped ribbon. The stripes represent water, earth and air – the naval, land and air forces. Established during World War Two by Maria Dickin CBE, founder of the PDSA (People's Dispensary for Sick Animals), the Dickin Medal was introduced to honour animals' devotion to man, and is awarded to animals displaying bravery in the line of duty while serving or associated with any branch of the armed forces or civil defence units.

Two dogs that earned the Dickin Medal in 2002 were Salty and Roselle, Labrador guide dogs. When the terrorist attack of 2001 was made on the World Trade Center on the now infamous date, 9/11, these remarkable dogs remained steadfastly by their blind owners' sides, bravely leading them down 70 floors to safety. Through smoke, mass panic and falling debris, the dogs did not falter. As well as receiving the Dickin Medal, Salty and Roselle were honoured by the UK's The Guide Dogs for the Blind Association.

DID YOU KNOW?

During the days of the Roman Empire teams of dogs were kitted out with armour or vicious spiked collars before being sent onto the battlefield to attack the enemy.

TAKING A BULLET

When a man suddenly appeared brandishing an AK-47 in Afghanistan in 2010, US Staff Sergeant John Mariana simply let his dog, Bronco, an eight-year-old Belgian Malinois, off his lead. The dog attacked the enemy, who retaliated by firing. Bronco ran off, and when Mariana found him he realised that Bronco had literally taken a bullet for him. Passing through the side of his mouth, the bullet had seriously damaged his muzzle and nose bone. The gutsy hound also had fractured teeth. After several gruelling surgeries, during which Mariana stayed by his dog's side, further surgery was needed back in America, so for five long months, man and dog were separated. When the pair were finally reunited both human and canine soldiers sobbed with joy. 'He worked for me because he loved me and I love him. And I really believe that he knew that,' Mariana is quoted as saying.

STUBBY THE HERO

One all-American Terrier brought great glory to the US army. He began as a stray wandering through an army training session at Yale Field in Connecticut in 1917, but quickly became friendly with all the soldiers. He was favoured especially by one soldier, Corporal Robert Conroy, who fell hook, line and sinker for the little dog. Christening him Stubby, most likely because of the size and shape of the dog's tail, it is said that the good Corporal Conroy was so fond of him that when he was posted to the Western Front he smuggled Stubby into France with him. Discovered too late to be returned, Stubby was permitted to stay with his master and became a part of the 102nd Infantry, 26th Division, known as the Yankee Division.

Plunged into the horrors of war the brave dog was present at battles including The Battle of Château-Thierry, the Marne and St Mihiel. He survived injuries from shrapnel and gas attacks, and is reported to have been so well-known for his guts and loyalty that he was treated like a proper soldier in Red Cross hospitals. He even brought down a German spy who attempted to tiptoe into the camp at night by biting his leg, which gave the troops time to imprison the intruder. Declared a hero, Stubby received more medals than any other soldier dog and was awarded lifetime membership of the American Legion.

His angry howl while a battle raged and his mad canter from one part of the lines to another indicated realization. But he seemed to know that the greatest service he could render was comfort and cheerfulness.

EXTRACT FROM STUBBY'S OBITUARY IN *THE NEW YORK TIMES* FOLLOWING HIS DEATH IN 1926

LOVE CONQUERS ALL

In addition to seeing active service, the companionship, affection and faithfulness that dogs have offered soldiers throughout history remains invaluable. Psychologically, the comforting presence of a dog is a welcome – essential, some would say – distraction from the grim brutality of war.

In recent conflict, Layla was found by a group of US Marines while on food patrol in Afghanistan. While the puppy had no military training to offer, she gave the soldiers one thing they desperately needed: love. Always ready to greet them with affection and a wagging tail when they returned to camp, she was an instant drop of canine sunshine that made their dangerous and highly pressurised circumstances more bearable.

The dog is a gentleman;
I hope to go to his
heaven not man's.

MARK TWAIN

NOT JUST BRAVE IN BATTLE

Using their wonderful noses to sniff out bombs, casualties, drugs and baddies, it's not just in battle that dogs save lives. Pet dogs have often been honoured for acts of heroism, when they have instinctively leapt to the defence of their human friends or alerted their families to imminent danger such as fire or, in 11-year-old Austin Forman's case, of prowling cougars.

When Austin went outside to collect wood for his family's wood-burning furnace at their home in British Columbia, Canada, Angel the 18-month-old Golden Retriever went with him. But the dog was acting out of character, and was cautious and obviously alert to something that Austin couldn't see. That's when a cougar tried to pounce on the boy. Leaping directly into the beast's path, Angel managed to fend it off until a local police constable arrived on the scene and shot it. Angel needed major surgery for head injuries but recovered well. Understandably, Austin was quick to empty his piggy bank and buy his Angel the biggest steak the butcher could supply.

SWIMMING SAVIOURS

Whilst on holiday with his family, black Labrador–Golden Retriever cross, Yaron, a guide dog, turned his paw to lifeguard duties. On the beach one day, one of the family's daughters, Charlotte, toppled off her bodyboard into the sea. Swept away by the current and with no lifejacket, she began to panic. Yaron jumped into the sea and began swimming towards her. Paddling in circles around her, enabling her to catch hold of his collar, Yaron calmly towed Charlotte safely back to shore. Yaron's heroics saw him named as the Beyond the Call of Duty Guide Dog of the Year 2008 at the American Guide Dog of the Year Awards.

DOCTOR DOG

In the spotlight during the American Society for the Prevention of Cruelty to Animals' Dog of the Year Awards in 2007, Toby the Golden Retriever from Maryland was recognised for his amazing lifesaving skills. When Toby's owner, Debbie Parkhurst, started to choke on a piece of apple she began to panic – the apple was lodged in her windpipe. When he saw that Debbie was struggling for breath, quick-thinking Toby performed the canine version of the Heimlich manoeuvre – he leapt hard onto her chest, forcing the wedged apple loose. Debbie owes her life to this amazing Doctor Dog.

DID YOU KNOW?

Barry, a St Bernard from Switzerland, is believed to be the breed's most successful rescuer, having saved more than 40 lives.

BITE-SIZED BRILLIANCE

Belle the Beagle from Florida is proof – if proof were needed – that dogs really are intelligent as well as loyal. When her diabetic owner, Kevin Weaver, had a seizure and collapsed in 2005, Belle's training as a diabetic assistance dog kicked straight in. Grabbing Kevin's mobile phone the little dog bit down on the number nine, the stored number for the emergency services. With his blood sugar having dropped to a potentially fatal level, Belle undoubtedly saved her owner's life – an act she was rightly honoured for when she became the first dog ever to win the VITA Wireless Samaritan Award, an award given to someone who has used a mobile telephone to save a life, prevent a crime or help in an emergency.

One day I hope to be the person my dog thinks I am.

ANONYMOUS

No animal I know of can consistently be more of a friend and companion than a dog.

STANLEY LEINWOLL

RESOURCES

Animal Search UK – www.animalsearchuk.co.uk

Association of Pet Behaviour Counsellors – www.apbc.org.uk

Battersea Dogs & Cats Home – www.battersea.org.uk

Bulldog Rescue & Rehoming Trust – www.bulldogrescue.org.uk

Canine Partners – www.caninepartners.org.uk

Dogs Trust – www.dogstrust.org.uk

German Shepherd Dog Rescue – www.germanshepherd rescue.co.uk

The Guide Dogs for the Blind Association – www.guidedogs.org.uk

Guild of Dog Trainers – www.godt.org.uk

Hearing Dogs for Deaf People – www.hearingdogs.org.uk

The Kennel Club – www.thekennelclub.org.uk

Labrador Retriever Rescue Southern England – www.labrador-rescue.org.uk

Lost and Stolen Dogs – www.doglost.co.uk

Medical Detection Dogs – www.medicaldetectiondogs.org.uk

Medivet Animal Trust (MAT) – www.ma-trust.org

People's Dispensary for Sick Animals (PDSA) – www.pdsa.org.uk

Poetic Dogs – www.danbannino.com/portfolio/poetic-dogs/

Retired Greyhound Trust – www.retiredgreyhounds.co.uk

Royal Society for the Prevention of Cruelty to Animals (RSPCA) – www.rspca.org.uk

Siberian Husky Club of Great Britain – www.siberianhuskyclub.org.uk

Support Dogs – www.supportdogs.org

FURTHER READING

Coile, Caroline *The Dog Breed Bible* (2007, Barron's)

Dilger, Andrew *Dash: Bitch of the Year* (2011, Summersdale)

Edward, Olivia *The More I See of Men, the More I Love My Dog* (2002, Summersdale)

Fogle, Bruce *RSPCA New Complete Dog Training Manual* (2006, Dorling Kindersley)

Fogle, Bruce *The New Encyclopedia of the Dog* (2000, Dorling Kindersley)

Hawkins, Barrie *Twenty Wagging Tales: Our Year of Rehoming Orphaned Dogs* (2009, Summersdale)

Holt, Ben *Wonder Dogs: True Stories of Canine Courage* (2017, Summersdale)

Jenkins, Garry *A Home of Their Own: The Heart-warming 150-year History of Battersea Dogs & Cats Home* (2010, Bantam Press)

Common, Jane *Phileas Dogg's Guide to Dog-Friendly Holidays in Britain* (2014, Constable)

Ward Keeble, Sharon *My Rescue Dog Rescued Me* (2016, Summersdale)

Webster, Richard *Is Your Pet Psychic? Developing Psychic Communication with Your Pet* (2015, Llewellyn Publications)

FOR THE LOVE OF CATS

Kate May

ISBN: 978 1 78685 031 7

£9.99

There are few things in life more heart-warming than to be welcomed by a cat.

TAY HOHOFF

They're intelligent, inquisitive, regal and daft. The smallest thing can spark their curious nature, they're always there when you need an extra cuddle, and with their soulful eyes and velvety paws, it's no wonder that cats are one of our most beloved animals.

PACKED WITH FASCINATING FACTS AND TRIVIA, HEART-WARMING STORIES AND INSPIRING QUOTES, *FOR THE LOVE OF CATS* IS PERFECT FOR ANYONE WHO KNOWS THE INCOMPARABLE JOY OF A PURRING FELINE COMPANION.

Have you enjoyed this book?
If so, why not write a review on your
favourite website?

If you're interested in finding out more
about our books, find us on Facebook at
Summersdale Publishers and follow us on
Twitter at @Summersdale.

Thanks very much for buying this
Summersdale book.

www.summersdale.com